Jesus special friends

Story by Penny Frank

Illustrated by John Haysom

Guideposts

34

CARMEL • NEW YORK 10512

The Bible tells how God sent his Son Jesus to show us what God is like and how we can belong to God's kingdom.

This is the story of how Jesus chose twelve men to be with him as he did God's special work.

You can find the story in your own Bible, in the first chapters of the Gospels of Mark and John.

Copyright © 1986 Lion Publishing

Published by
Lion Publishing plc
Icknield Way, Tring, Herts, England
Lion Publishing Corporation
1705 Hubbard Avenue, Batavia,
Illinois 60510, USA
Albatross Books Pty Ltd
PO Box 320, Sutherland, NSW 2232, Australia

First edition 1986
Reprinted 1986

British Library Cataloguing in Publication Data

Frank, Penny
  Jesus' special friends. – (The Lion
  Story Bible; 34)
  1. Apostles – Juvenile literature
  2. Bible stories, English. N.T.
  Gospels
  I. Title   II. Haysom, John
  226′.0922   BS2440

Library of Congress Cataloging in Publication Data

Frank, Penny.
Jesus' special friends.
(The Lion Story Bible; 34)
1. Apostles – Biography – Juvenile
literature.
2. Biblo. N.T. – Biography – Juvenile
literature.
3. Bible stories, English – N.T.
Gospels. [1. Apostles. 2. Jesus Christ.
3. Bible stories – N.T.] I. Haysom,
John, ill. II. Title. III. Series: Frank,
Penny. Lion Story Bible; 34.
BS2440.F693 1986   226′.309505
85-15955

Printed and bound in Hong Kong by Mandarin Offset International (HK) Ltd
This Guideposts edition is published by special arrangement with Lion Publishing

As Jesus grew up, he often listened to
people talking about his cousin, John.
   He knew that John was a preacher
who lived by the River Jordan.
All the people went to listen to him.

'God is sending his Son to be your king,'
John told them. 'But you are not
ready for him. You are God's special
people but you do not do as he says.'

The people knew that was true. They often broke God's laws. They found it hard to be good.

'We really are sorry,' they said. 'What shall we do?'

'Come and be baptized in the river,' said John, 'to show everyone that you really do want your life to be clean and good. And God will forgive you.'

Hundreds of people went to John to be baptized. They called him John the Baptist.

Although Jesus had done nothing wrong, he too went to be baptized with all the people. When Jesus came up out of the river they heard a voice, saying:

'You are my own dear Son. I am pleased with you.'

Jesus knew that it was time to begin God's work. It would be hard. So he went away on his own to the desert hills to think and pray.

He had nothing to eat for many days.

But Satan, the enemy who had spoiled
God's world, wanted to stop Jesus
from doing God's work.

He waited until Jesus was alone
and very hungry.

Then Satan tried every way he could
to make Jesus obey him, instead of God.

But Jesus said, 'I will never serve you,
Satan. God's word says I must serve
only him.'

So, in the end, Satan went away. But
Jesus knew that he would never give up.

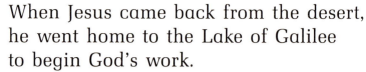

When Jesus came back from the desert,
he went home to the Lake of Galilee
to begin God's work.

He saw two men fishing on the lake.

'Simon! Andrew!' Jesus called. 'Come
with me! We'll go and find people for
the kingdom of God, instead of fish
for the market.'

Then Jesus saw two more fishermen,
sitting in their boat, cleaning the nets.

'James! John!' Jesus called. 'Come on,
I need you too.'

The four fishermen left everything by
the lake and went with Jesus.

The next person Jesus chose to work with him was Philip. He came from Bethsaida, the same town as Simon and Andrew.

Philip was very excited when Jesus invited him to join them. He hurried to tell Nathanael all about it.

'No one important comes from Nazareth!' said Nathanael.

But he went with Philip to meet Jesus.

'Hello, Nathanael,' said Jesus. 'I saw you sitting under that fig-tree before Philip called you!'

Jesus knew all about him! So Nathanael went with Jesus too.

One day Jesus and his special friends were invited to a wedding, at Cana in Galilee.

Mary, the mother of Jesus, was helping with the wedding feast, because she knew the bride very well.

All the guests wore their best clothes.
Everyone was very excited and happy.
   The tables for the feast were bright
with flowers and the bride looked
really beautiful.

They were all enjoying themselves,
when Jesus saw Mary looking worried.
'What is the matter?' he asked gently.

'Oh dear,' said Mary. 'This is terrible. The shame of it! People will never let us forget it. We have run out of wine. Will you help?'

Mary shook the arm of the chief servant.

'Do exactly what my son says,' she told him.

'Take those six huge jars,' Jesus said
to him, 'and fill them to the very top
with water.'

The servant did as he was told, but he
was not happy. They did not want water
to drink at a wedding.

When the jars were all full, Jesus said,
'Now pour some out and take it to the
most important guest.'

When the servant obeyed, he nearly
dropped the cup. It was full of wine!

'That's the best wine I've ever tasted,'
said the guest.

It was Jesus' first miracle, the first
of many wonderful things he did.

When Jesus went back to the Lake of Galilee, many people went with him. They had heard about the miracle at the wedding. They did not want to miss anything exciting.

They went past the place where the tax
man was sitting.

'Hey, Matthew!' called out Jesus.
'Leave all that money and come with me.
I need you.'

So Matthew got up and left
everything. He joined the group of Jesus'
special friends.

Jesus chose twelve of his followers to be his special friends. They were with him all the time. They listened when he told the people God's message. They were called the twelve apostles.

Here are their names:
Simon Peter and his brother Andrew,
James and his brother John,
Philip and Bartholomew,
Thomas and Matthew, the tax man,
another James, and Thaddaeus,
Simon the Patriot
and Judas Iscariot.

The Story Bible Series from Guideposts is made up of 50 individual stories for young readers, building up an understanding of the Bible as one story—God's story—a story for all time and all people.

The Old Testament story books tell the story of a great nation—God's chosen people, the Israelites—and God's love and care for them through good times and bad. The stories are about people who knew and trusted God. From this nation came one special person, Jesus Christ, sent by God to save all people everywhere.

The New Testament story books cover the life and teaching of God's Son, Jesus. The stories are about the people he met, what he did and what he said. Almost all we know about the life of Jesus is recorded in the four Gospels—Matthew, Mark, Luke and John. The word gospel means 'good news.'

The last four stories in this section are about the first Christians, who started to tell others the 'good news,' as Jesus had commanded them—a story which continues today all over the world.

The story of *Jesus' special friends* comes from the New Testament, Mark's Gospel chapters 1 to 3, and John's Gospel chapters 1 and 2. At the beginning of his special work for God, Jesus identified himself with his people by being baptized. Unlike everyone else he had done no wrong. He did not need a new start. He simply did what God wanted. And as he came out of the water God declared himself pleased with Jesus. God had given him great power but Jesus knew it must be used to help others, not himself. He stood firm against every temptation Satan could conjure up. He answered him in the Bible's own words. Then he went home to Galilee and began to choose his special band of followers — the twelve.